SCRAPPING THE SCRUBS:
A GUIDE FOR NURSE
ENTREPRENEURS
Michelle Mattson

Dedication

This book is written for those of you who are frustrated, feeling overworked, and ready for something new, yet have no idea on how to even begin. It is my hope that in reading this, you get the sense that you are in control, you just need to pivot your path into a different direction. With some research, planning, and hard work, you can make a choice to change the course of your career.

Acknowledgements

This book would not be possible if not for the continual encouragement of my nurse friends, family, and former co-workers. Thank you to the nurse entrepreneur peers I have met along the way and those who have contributed to this book. Most importantly, a special thank you to my husband Eric, for your continued support of me through all of my adventures in life.

"Whatever you can do, or dream you can, begin it. Boldness has genius, power and magic in it."

Johann Wolfgang von Goethe

Nurses are taught how to perform many tasks such as how to assess their patients, how to calculate drug dosages, and how to document. We are not taught how to be business owners.

Michelle Mattson

Be bold enough to challenge your station and move to a better place. Be bold enough to believe in yourself.

Author Unknown

PREFACE

Many nurses go into healthcare because they genuinely care for people. Others choose this profession because they sense job security as people will always get sick, hurt, and need medical attention. After a certain period, you may find yourself no longer fulfilled. Staffing shortages, shift work, holidays, and increased demands are all reasons nurses decide to leave the bedside. There is nothing wrong with deciding that direct patient care in the traditional sense is no longer for you. If you have decided that you are no longer fulfilled, I encourage you to pursue other avenues. You are not doing anyone any favors by staying in a position that you do not enjoy, and often your dissatisfaction will become evident to your patients. While it is certainly unfair for a patient to be impacted by an unhappy nurse, it is also unfair to you and your own happiness for you to continue working somewhere that does not fit who you are. Sometimes people change. Sometimes the role itself changes. Maybe you think that nursing isn't "you" anymore.

The idea for this book came about in the summer of 2019 as I reviewed some of the mistakes I have made along the way as I started my own business. I realized that some of the information on how to start a business was hard to find. I put the book on hold in 2020 for personal reasons and did not revisit it until we were well into the pandemic in 2021. I am back because I feel compelled to share this information for those of you who are now feeling burned out. Healthcare is a very stressful and at times physical environment. Add on top of it the pandemic stressors of shortages in PPE, patients dying without family, short staffing due to sickness, and now the normal stressors are multiplied. This book is for you, the aging nurse who can no longer keep up with the physical demands of the frontlines. This book is for you, the younger nurse who now has a family and shift work is not conducive to family life. This book is for you, the frontline workers who no longer feel committed to your current role for whatever reason.

Table of Contents

INTRODUCTION

We all get to a point in our lives where we start to question our choices, our career paths, and our future. For some, it occurs sooner than later. Some ponder their options curiously but do not act on the other paths that they identify. Some dream but do not make the changes necessary to fulfill their dreams. Others, well, let's just say there are those of us who will not let anyone define us by a title, or a predefined path.

Like me, many of you graduated from your professional training programs excited and ready to conquer the world. You were excited to have a badge with your credentials clearly displayed. You were nervous on the job but excited to learn more every day that you returned. Somehow, you may have lost the spark. Maybe it was lost long ago, maybe it was missing so many family events, or maybe it was the pandemic that did you in.

In the back of my mind, I always had an entrepreneurial spirit. I always thought it would be the most amazing thing to work for yourself. I doubted whether I could really pull it off. In fact, if you asked me three years ago, I would never have imagined that I would have done it.

One day, after pondering the idea for a few months, I decided it was time.

If you are reading this book, you are most likely dissatisfied with your station in life. Perhaps you are feeling overworked, underpaid, unappreciated, and physically and mentally burned out. If this is the case, you are not alone. Hundreds, if not thousands, of nurses walk away from the traditional roles every year. Some retire. Others still need to work but just cannot stomach another day working on the floor. After the pandemic, many more nurses may decide to leave the bedside, potentially more than in previous years. If you choose to walk away from the traditional setting, you are not necessarily giving up nursing, what you are doing is envisioning your nursing career differently.

It is my hope that while reading this book you will use it as a career care plan of sorts. Remember the nursing process and care plans? Working through the different sections of this book will be like using the nursing process to lay out how you will become an entrepreneur.

Assessment- You will assess why you want to move away from your current role.

Diagnosis- What do you diagnose as the reason for wanting to start a business, based on the above assessment?

Planning- Based on the above, you will plan a strategy to get your business started.

Implementation/Intervention- You will begin to implement steps to get yourself on your way to becoming a business owner.

Evaluation- After your business is up and running, you will need to continually evaluate each of the above components, just as you would evaluate a patient's progress, you will evaluate your business's progress. Reassess.

CHAPTER 1- WHY

Why would you want to work for yourself? Most of us probably grew up with the idea that we would just go to school, learn a trade, or earn a degree, and then go work for a company who would provide us with a paycheck every two weeks. This has been the traditional "work" that many of our parents did. So, why would you want to give up the idea of a guaranteed paycheck every two weeks? Isn't it easy to just show up and do what you are asked to do, and then go home? For many, the answer is yes. If you are reading this book, perhaps you are not part of the many but part of the few, willing to take a risk on yourself. Maybe you had not given it any thought until now.

Working for yourself will not be easy. In fact, you will be the most demanding boss, and quite possibly your harshest critic. The rewards of working for yourself, proving that you are more than "just a nurse" (not that there's anything wrong with being a nurse), and making money on your own terms is the most exciting and fulfilling adventure that you will experience. The satisfaction gained by growing a business from concept to reality is one that will be filled with pride. You can do this!

New businesses are started every day all over the country. If others can do it, so can you. Here is a statistic for you: despite the pandemic, the U.S. Census Bureau claims that in the first three quarters of 2020, over 3.2 million new business applications were initiated. For comparison in 2019, only 2.7 million were initiated. Perhaps many are using this time to re-invent themselves and maybe the time is right for you as well.

Being a nurse entrepreneur has the value of giving you what a traditional employment arrangement often cannot:

Freedom. With certain limitations, depending on the type of business you enter, you are free to work when you want and take time off when you want. You are the boss of you.

Satisfaction. The satisfaction of working for yourself, building your own empire, and watching it grow is like nothing you have ever experienced before. We work 200 times harder when it is our own business than we ever would for someone else. While entrepreneurial ventures are not a solution to solving a work-life balance issue, the satisfaction can be well worth it if you accept this path with the right attitude and a little patience.

Personal growth. Owning, running, and being successful in your own business will at times keep you up at night. You will want to quit. You will have highs and lows and be scared out of your mind. You will also grow in so many ways that I cannot even begin to explain. It changes you. This journey might be just what you need to fully experience your perceived professional worth.

The above are just a few things to be gained from working for yourself. I do not know which, if any, of those factors motivate or scare you (they should do both, by the way). I do not know you and you do not know me.

My "Why"

I cannot tell your story, but let me give you some insight into mine. The "why" decision came for me when I just got tired of working for an employer who did not value me as a professional, my contributions, or my loyalty. I think overall he looked down on anyone that was a nurse as if it was a demeaning profession.

I was working in a high-level management position for a small startup company with locations in several states. In the beginning, my work required me to travel locally within my state and within just a few hours radius from my home base. My responsibilities included oversight of the clinical operations at our local facilities. Within the first year, things quickly changed, and I found myself traveling across the country, often on short notice, and staying on site at various locations for weeks, and sometimes months at a time with little travel home. There was no balance between my work and family life. I was called at 5 am and at 9 pm, with no consideration given to my personal life or the sacrifices that were being made by my family. I missed the birth of my granddaughter.

I began to reach my boiling point after my second Christmas season away from home. Upon asking for a bonus and not getting one, I found out that one of my subordinates asked for a raise and got it (meaning she was making more money than me), yet I was doing half of her job for her. My disgust meter hit full and I knew that my career with this company would surely be over before the next holiday season rolled around.

Layoffs, terminations, and struggles at the company continued. Two years in and my job felt like a bad marriage that I could not get out of. The pay was good, but the sacrifices of my time, my soul, my spirit, and my family were not worth the golden handcuffs. I knew I had to get out, but I also knew that I needed a challenge. I had to come up with a plan.

Fast forward to the following summer, and the idea of working independently is still swirling around in my head. My boss had just gotten intolerable, his expectations unreasonable, and my faith in the failing company had reached rock bottom. I had enough of the antics and was finally ready to do something for me. I had persevered long enough and had to make a move.

I knew a few colleagues who worked for themselves. They seemed very happy with the freedom of being their own bosses. Knowing that they were able to pull it off successfully gave me hope. In thinking about it, I knew that I always had an independent streak, and accomplished whatever I had set my mind to in the past.

I decided that my business would be similar to the type of work that I was doing while an employee, but I would work for myself and my own company. As scary as it sounded, I thought the worst that could happen is that I would have to go back into the job market. At least I could try to work for myself. Nothing ventured, nothing gained.

A month before my last day of employment, I began forming my company, reviewing sample contracts, and making sure my finances were in order. Once I jumped off the cliff, I was going to hit the water with a splash. I could not do a belly flop.

What I did not know at the time was anything about the local market where I lived, since I was relatively new to the area. I also did not know that with my new business providing on-site services, the pandemic would drastically impact my ability to work. I'm not trying to scare you away, I am telling you this early on so that you know that my business struggled, and that I did not do everything right. I do not see this as a failure because if I can inspire, scare, and challenge you, maybe you will be in a better place starting your endeavor.

What can you do? Before you can decide what you can do, it may be helpful to decide why you want to leave. There is no right or wrong answer to this question. Perhaps you want to quit your job because you do not enjoy the work. You might be an introvert and find that you do not function well in environments which require tact, patience, and constant collaboration. If this is you, then determining your path may require you to find a role where you will not have patient interaction. In this sense, your customers most likely will not be patients and you would not want to start a service-based business. Of course, you are not prohibited from starting some type of service business, but just know that you will still have patient interactions.

Perhaps you are an aging nurse and you cannot physically keep up with the demands of the role, so you would explore less physically demanding options.

Perhaps you love being a nurse and the interactions with patients and families but you perceive that your role does not allow you the ability to provide the personal touches to your patients that attracted you to nursing in the first place.

As I stated earlier in the Introduction, what you are doing in this step is an assessment of your situation, your reason, your why. The assessment will continue as we move further, and you assess your skills.

Later on in the book, we will go into detail on setting up the business and factors to consider when getting started. Before we can get there, you will need to make some other decisions as these determinants impact the structure and pricing of your business.

While making the decision to start working for yourself is the first step, naturally, you will need an idea of what type of business you want to start. Will you work a service-based business, sell a product or many products? Before you can drill down to that level, you must decide a little about how you best work, what excites you, what drains you, etc. What do you have to offer that may have value to others?

Before you begin to make these discoveries, take a step back and get to know yourself a little better.

Do you feel like you have settled for safe or comfortable?

Do you fear letting others down if you decide to change course and follow your dreams?

Have you put your dreams on hold until your children are grown or your financial situation changes?

Do you feel like you are living on someone else's terms?

Are you concerned with what others think of you or your ability?

Are you afraid of criticism or rejection?

Regarding your career:

Do you feel like at some point during your career, you were happy with your role?

If you answered yes, what were you doing at that point in your career? What did you like about it? What did you dislike about it?

Thinking back to this point in your career where you were happy, what was your personal life like? Has your personal life changed?

Use the above questions to determine whether you were truly happy in your career. Reflect and determine whether you were happy in the role, or just happy with your personal situation.

If your personal situation has not changed, and you still believe you were at one point happy in your career, determine what made you happy about that particular role, and that particular time. Below are some more questions to help you discover yourself.

Are you an introvert or extrovert?

Are you organized or scattered?

Are you better with structure or without structure?

Are there aspects of your current role that you are particularly good at?

Do you like paperwork, planning, and administrative type work?

Do you enjoy the more social aspect of your work?

Do you have many years of experience in a certain specialty?

Are you more drawn to creative work?

What are your hobbies, and can any of these be transformed into a business?

Have you thought about a service, or product that you wish existed? Is there a product or service that does exist, but you feel is lacking?

After you have established answers to these questions, look at the skills that you perform in your current role and determine if any of these skills are items that you enjoy doing and would enjoy doing in a different environment.

Below are a few skills that nurses have:

Educator- Educating patients and families on proper care, after care (post procedures, etc.) to name a few. Educating other team members on procedures, processes, preceptorship, providing study tips for certification (if you are certified in that specialty), etc. Do you enjoy this part of your work?

Counselor- Nurses act as counselors when they listen to their patients and allow them to express their feelings, concerns, etc. We act as counselors through leadership positions as we counsel staff members. Do you enjoy this part of your work?

Negotiators- Nurses act as negotiators, persuading our patients to get up and walk after surgery even though they don't want to. Nurses persuade doctors that there is "something" just not right about a patient although their vitals look fine. Are you exceptionally gifted at persuasion?

Analyst- Some nursing roles have tasks which require data analysis, compiling data, and creating reports with the results. Is this a task that you enjoy performing? Do you enjoy analyzing and solving problems?

Strategic planner- Do you have to strategize the best way to accomplish your daily tasks? Do you enjoy planning complex projects? Do you enjoy being on a team that strategizes and plans projects?

Research- Do you conduct research as part of your role? Do you enjoy reading and writing reports based on the findings of your research?

Writer- Are you creative? Do you flourish in thinking outside the box? Can you think of ways to transition into roles where your background can be used creatively?

Health and Wellness- Are you a health and wellness enthusiast? Do you find yourself always encouraging your family to eat better, sleep more, reduce stress, and exercise more? Can you find a way to transition your nursing skills into this area?

The possibilities are endless, and hopefully you are getting an idea of how there are a variety of skills that come with nursing roles. Below is an exercise that may help you get a little more clarity.

Using TABLE A below, list your skills and traits in either the positive or negative columns based on whether you view them as positive or negative. The table approach will help you identify those areas of your current situation which you view as positive (and will be useful in developing your business ideas) or negative (meaning that they may not serve you in your business).

Skills

Conduct an assessment of your skills beginning with your current work experience, making a list of the skills that you are using in your current position. During this process, you should be looking for keywords that describe what you do on a daily basis in your job.

Traits

Conduct an assessment of traits that are transferable based on the type of nursing job that you currently have. For example, if you are a case manager or nurse navigator, a trait that you might have is that you enjoy interacting with people. If you are a critical care nurse, a trait that you might have is that you are very structured, detail-oriented, and perhaps are more introverted.

Once the table has been completed, you should have an idea of what skills and traits are transferable and could serve you well in another form of business.

Table A- Your Skills and Traits

Positive	Negative

After you complete the above table, ask your co-workers what they think are your skills and traits. Add them to the list if they are not on there already. Often, we do not give ourselves credit, so those working closest to you might view your abilities differently than you do.

Example:

Katie is an oncology nurse navigator. She spends her days coordinating patient care and explaining what the chemotherapy process will be like for her newly diagnosed cancer patients.

Positive	Negative
Enjoys the relationship she forms with her patients.	She finds it sad and emotionally draining to watch her patients struggle with their new diagnosis.
She is proficient in coordinating multiple schedules and tasks.	She doesn't like computers.
She is organized.	

After reviewing the example given and coming up with your own list, the next step is to look at your hobbies and outside interests to determine if any of these are business-worthy options.

Take your hobbies and interests and place them in TABLE B below.

In your spare time, what do you enjoy doing? Are you someone who prefers to be active, are you artistic, or do you spend your spare time reading, and discovering new concepts?

If you like to read, what do you enjoy reading and learning about? Health and wellness, different cultures, fiction, non-fiction, science?

Is there a particular population that you would prefer to spend your time with, young children, young adults, middle aged adults, elderly adults, families?

Table B- Your Hobbies and Interests

Subject	Specifics

Example:

Here, Katie lists her hobbies and interests.

Subject	Specifics
Reading	Relationships and self-help books
Enjoys listening to music.	Likes classical music
Enjoys entertaining.	Loves to coordinate parties.

Now that you have listed your skills, traits, hobbies, and interests, you must ask your family and friends outside of your work environment what they honestly think are your skills and traits. What hobbies do they think you are good at? Compare and add anything to the tables if they are not already there. Again, we need an accurate assessment. We can be hard on ourselves so get feedback from others.

Once you have completed the assessments, it is now time to look at other ideas. Have you found the need for a particular product or service that is not already in existence, or is not well represented in your geographical area? List those in the space below:

Services or Products	In existence: Yes or No	Comments

If you have found that there are products or services that are in existence but not well represented, you will need to spend some time doing research on the competition.

During the interview process with other nurse entrepreneurs, I have discovered that many of these nurses have identified a product or service which was lacking in the marketplace.

We talked about the nursing process in the beginning of the book. While it may not seem obvious, after you have completed the assessment of your situation, you can come up with a diagnosis of what the problem or issue is with your current situation after using the above tools.

Lisa Porter, the creator of JobDocs, is what she calls an "accidental entrepreneur" as she was wishing there was an application to store her licensing and credentialing documents on her phone in a way that would allow her to keep up with expiration dates. There was not an application, so she created it. She assessed the situation, diagnosed that there wasn't a solution and then implemented a plan to create it!

The same story holds true for Brian Mohika, founder of Cathwear, and Joey Ferry, co-creator of SafeSeizure pads. These products were not in existence to their satisfaction and so created the ideal product. Assessment, Diagnosis, Implementation!!!!

The above are just three wonderful examples of our fellow nurses making an impact in the business world. You can do the same thing once you complete all the required steps and create a well-crafted plan for success. There are many options of businesses for nurses to start. Below, we will break down the various types.

A service-based business, one where you are selling yourself as the service provider, will be the easiest and most cost effective to start. You will not have the overhead of manufacturing or inventory but will still have some startup costs as with any business. There will be inherent limits on the workload and income related to this type of business because there is only one "you" and only so many hours in a week. Of course, this does not mean you should not consider this option. Just know you are time limited and if you are the only employee, you will run out of hours or will need to hire someone else to delegate tasks to. Examples of service type businesses are consulting businesses, patient advocates, case managers, foot service businesses, and health coaches to name a few.

Heather Wilson, founder of Everyday Divinity, identified a service that was not provided in the marketplace for her area. If you identify a service that is not provided in your area, be sure to do the research to determine if there is a true need for that service. As I stated in my story, my consulting business was not one in high demand in the area that I lived due to most health systems, surgery centers, and medical practices belonging to 1 of 2 large health systems in the area, requiring me to travel to conduct my business.

The second type of business is a product business. This type may be the hardest to start as there will be more up-front costs (to manufacture a product). This business has more growth potential since you are not selling your time in exchange for revenue. The product will take more time to develop as it takes time through trial and error to get the product right. Lisa Porter, Joey Ferry, and Brian Mohika all created product businesses.

The third type of business is a knowledge business. This type of business is one in which you are converting what you know into a product such as a course, study guide, or other media/print work. This option also can be more scalable than a service-based business in which you are the actual service provider.

Hopefully, you are on the right path of thinking about things you enjoy, things you are good at, and things you do not enjoy. Be mindful, however, that it is not enough to just be good at something as you might find yourself bored or in a failed business. It is also not enough to enjoy something but not be talented at it, as ultimately you will not receive the success you intend. Identifying the ideal business should be done with deliberation, time, and patience.

I speak from the heart when I tell you that you must really explore potential ideas carefully. When I started working for myself, I might have reconsidered the business I started if I had done a little more research on the local market. It may sound funny that the person writing this book to help you start your own business is telling you that she made a mistake.

I did not make a mistake; I learned a few valuable lessons which I hope you can learn from:

The whole idea of having a better work life balance did not work out the way I had hoped due to the nature of my business- I am the service.

While I can take days off, if I do not work I do not get paid, because I am the service.

The market for my services in my geographical area was not what I had thought it was causing me to continue to travel away from my family to provide my services. A better study of the market may have prevented me from starting the service business at the time that I started it. I may have decided to relocate before starting the business or offer a different type of service. I allowed my emotions, exhaustion, and desire to be in control of my life drive my decisions.

Geographically and economically speaking, travel from my state of residence is time consuming and at times pricey. These factors impact both my free time (traveling to/from clients) and can impact my customers in terms of travel expenses and ultimately what they are willing to pay me (price). The pandemic has slowed down travel quite a bit. Due to the nature of my business, it was not one that could easily be done remotely. Again, I am the service and parts of my service cannot be performed off site.

I am not unhappy that I started my business, do not get me wrong. I love entrepreneurship. I have learned so much I never would have known had I not gone down this path. I have also connected with numerous entrepreneurs which has given me courage as I learn that we all fight similar battles. Some of these battles include doubting yourself and the fear of being rejected. Entrepreneurship is lonely at times and having other like-minded professionals to support you is key.

Self-exploration is critical in getting this right. The opportunities are endless but you must be willing to think about it, really get down deep into who you are and what you are. Do not let preconceived ideas of what nurses do keep you in an unfulfilled situation. Be sure to take your time and explore all possibilities for an extended period before you leave your employer.

CHAPTER 3-THE DECISION

If you are still reading this book, then there is a chance that you have an independent spirit and may do well as an entrepreneur. As scary as it sounds, maybe the idea of not working another 12-hour shift without meals or bathroom breaks is starting to sound possible. You have made the decision to keep reading and envision a career with possibilities. Over the next chapters, we will use the next steps in the nursing process, planning and implementation (intervention).

Part of the decision-making process includes putting a plan of action into place. The action plan needs to include:

Identifying your business idea. Most likely you will start with several ideas and then narrow those down. The previous chapter should help you get started on ideas based on your abilities and background.

Assess your financial situation. Are you part of a two-income household which might give you the ability to reduce your current work schedule allowing more time to focus on ramping up your business?

Will money be an issue while you are getting your business setup? For most the answer is yes. Does your spouse or partner support your efforts to work independently and are they willing to buckle down and forego the lattes to help ease the financial burden of a reduced income? This may sound silly, but do you have things around the house that you can sell to raise capital? You would be surprised at how much money those dumbbells or that unused treadmill sitting in your garage might be worth, especially during these times. Clean out your closets, garage, and attic. Look for valuable items that you don't need anymore. Raising capital can be good for seed money to open your business account, or use to pay off debt, freeing you from your miserable job sooner. Think outside the box on ways to get your finances in order if that is what is keeping you from living a happier, more fulfilled life.

If you are single, are you able to either take in a roommate, or move in with family to reduce your monthly overhead? Cutting down your housing costs can either get you out of debt faster or fatten up your bank account quicker allowing you to get out of a bad situation faster.

If your current financial situation is a challenge, outline a strategy which may get you in a better financial situation. Unfortunately for some, this may require picking up extra shifts to assist in reducing debt or to assist you in creating a cash cushion to fund your business. While this sounds controversial to the whole idea of working for yourself, if you cannot afford to quit your job, take immediate action to change your situation. Do not just up and quit.

Can you start your business as a side hustle on your off days? This is often the least risky path and if it is doable depending on your work schedule, this option is often highly recommended. Keeping one foot in the door is a lot safer than just quitting and scrambling. I highly recommend at least maintaining per diem status somewhere to keep yourself actively practicing nursing. This is just my opinion, but nursing is one career area where it appears that taking any time away from active nursing makes it more difficult to find work later, should the need arise. I am not saying that I agree, but there appears to be a misconception in nursing that if you leave the bedside for a few years, you suddenly are no longer able to perform nursing functions. I completely disagree with this theory, but do yourself a favor and try to keep at least "a toe" in nursing.

Volunteer work as a nurse may satisfy this requirement and is worth considering.

Keep your eyes on the prize. Once you make the decision and are clear to work for yourself, you need a roadmap on how to get there.

You will need mentors. You cannot do this on your own. If you have trusted family and friends who can act as your sounding board, great. You should also seek mentors in the business community; former colleagues with the expertise you need, connections met through networking, other entrepreneurs. The Small Business Administration/SCORE has offices nationwide and they enlist volunteer mentors who are usually retired business executives, and they can be of great assistance to you. The SCORE mentors come from many different fields that are not necessarily healthcare so they cannot help you with nursing related issues. I suggest consulting with nurse colleagues who can help you with specific nursing type questions. The National Nurses In Business Association (NNBA) is a great network offering support, information, and collaboration for nurse entrepreneurs.
A business coach or mentor can help you along the way as you work through tough decisions. They can also be neutral and provide you objective information that you, the business

owner, cannot see. The coach can be valuable to you in setting up the business, helping you assess your product, strategy, and structure.

The financial decisions and life impact of starting an entrepreneurial business is further reaching than just the obvious questions surrounding funding. When making these decisions, you will need to consider the tax implications, medical coverage decisions, as well as other benefits that a typical employer relationship covers. I am not an expert in any of these fields, so I will just provide a high-level overview of things to take into consideration.

Tax Implications

One important aspect to be considered when you step out on your own is the fact that you will no longer have an employer withholding federal, state, and social security tax from your paychecks. You will be responsible for ensuring that you pay your own taxes on a quarterly basis depending on your business structure. Once I started my consulting business, I calculated that approximately 30% of my gross revenue would need to be allocated to pay for my federal and state taxes. Calculating and reserving a percentage of your revenue for tax purposes is extremely important. I calculate my fees based on the 30% rule which I consider my markup to cover employer and employee withholding amounts. I charge 30% more than my desired take home pay to offset the self-employment taxes I will owe.

An example:

Perhaps you have a service-based business and your normal hourly rate for work is $40 per hour, your billable rate to a client ideally should be $57 per hour to compensate for taxation purposes, or otherwise you are losing money by working for yourself. If this amount sounds unreasonable, then consider a markup of at least 15% to cover the employer withholding portion that you will now be responsible for. In that regard, you could get away with charging $48 per hour to net $40 per hour. This covers the employer portion only and you will still owe the employee portion of your taxes which could put you in a bind at tax time. Since I am not a CPA, I will not go into too much detail on this topic. Bottom line, take into consideration that the rate you charge per hour either needs to cover for your tax liabilities or you are losing money by working for yourself.

Health Insurance

If you are working for yourself, health insurance is a topic to consider. If you have a spouse that can provide insurance coverage this is an option to take advantage of.

If you are reducing your status or leaving a full-time job completely and you have the option to enroll in your spouse's coverage, this is considered a qualifying life event, which allows you to enroll in employer sponsored coverage outside of the typical open enrollment period. This is a more affordable option than the options I will cover next.

For those of you whom the above option does not apply, consider applying for COBRA health insurance through your employer. To get a rough idea of what COBRA insurance costs, look at your paystub and view the employee pre-tax contribution amount and multiply by 3. You will pay this amount if not slightly more per month for your health coverage should you elect the COBRA option. In my experience, COBRA coverage for an individual can run between $1200 and $1800 per month, so this option is costly. Electing COBRA coverage will provide you with health coverage for approximately 18 months which will give you time to evaluate other options, even if you only do this in the short term.

Marketplace plans are available for those who choose not to elect COBRA coverage. Understand that many of these plans are affordable but have high deductibles. Preventative care is usually covered with a small or no co-pay. Keep in mind that in the event that you experience a serious illness or injury, you will most likely pay for most of your medical care (due to the high deductibles) before the payer will pay any benefit. Typically, the more you can afford to pay monthly, the lower the deductible before your coverage kicks in.

Healthcare.gov is a good place to start if you are looking for marketplace insurance coverage. Some insurance brokers will also work with you to assist you in finding healthcare insurance. I have worked with a few nurses who made most of their income through agency work and elected to get coverage on their own through an independent licensed broker.

Healthcare ministries are another option to consider. While I do not personally know anyone that has used these options, they exist. These are essentially cost sharing communities in which members pool their money monthly and use it to cover member's health expenses. Often these are faith-based ministries and may have limitations on who can become a member. An internet search for health-sharing ministries will provide you a starting point for research.

Whichever option you choose, understand that there are no longer tax penalties for not having health insurance. You are encouraged as a professional to be responsible for maintaining your health and health coverage.

Lastly, I encourage you to consult a tax professional regarding this, but typically, health insurance premiums paid by a self-employed individual may be considered a deductible business expense which may lower the overall taxable income of your business.

CHAPTER 4- STRATEGY AND STRUCTURE

We have covered things to consider when deciding to venture out on your own. Now it is time to move on to strategy and structure.

Strategy

Once I made the decision to head down the entrepreneurial path, I began by formulating an approach. My initial strategy was to perform the same type of work independently. I spent time studying information on how to formulate consulting contracts and started drafting samples. I needed time to set up shop before I would be fully prepared so my strategy was to turn in a 30-day notice after I had created my business, completed research on how to contract, and was ready. Timelines for your individual strategies may vary, but my best advice is that you continue in your current work while you set up your business and conduct your research in your off hours. Often, it is a best practice to continue working in your regular job for a period as you are getting your business off the ground if you are able to. Do the right thing and DO NOT WORK ON YOUR BUSINESS while at your full-time job.

If your intention and situation allows you to quit your full-time job, plan well in advance. Save up any remaining PTO/vacation days if you are able to and put that money aside for when you do not have an income. Plan any doctor visits while you still have your employer health coverage. Begin networking to expand your social and professional network prior to leaving your current job. Plan, Plan, and Plan!

Consider your strategy as an integral part of your new business roadmap. You wouldn't plan a road trip without making reservations, packing, and planning in advance would you?

Business Structure

You will need to determine what kind of business to set up; a corporation (C-corp, S-corp), an LLC (limited liability corporation), or work as an independent contractor using 1099 status with your clients. The U.S. Small Business Administration (SBA) is an excellent resource for obtaining information on the various types of businesses. You can find this information on the internet at www.sba.gov.

Register

You may need to register your business with the state if you are not using the 1099 option (which uses your social security number for clients). If you are starting a business that is not based on using a 1099 status, you will need to register your business with the IRS and obtain a TAX ID/EIN (Employer Identification number). The Small Business Administration has very helpful information on their website in regards to this process.

https://www.sba.gov/business-guide/10-steps-start-your-business

Registered Agent

I highly recommend working with a registered agent. A registered agent serves as the business point of contact if there is an unfortunate circumstance requiring you to be involved with legal proceedings. If you choose to list yourself and your private residence as the point of contact for a business, then you are subjecting your personal address to the public. A registered agent can accept documents on your behalf through their respective offices. The fee for a registered agent is usually a few hundred dollars per year.

You can learn more about a registered agent on this website:

https://www.score.org/resource/should-you-hire-registered-agent-or-be-your-own

Banking

Set up a checking account and a savings account for your business. This is very crucial in keeping your business monies separate from your personal monies. To set up banking, you will need to provide the bank with your business license and TAX ID/EIN number. Credit unions and small local banks are good options for your business as they typically charge less in service charges than large institutions.

If you have listened to the news recently, you may have heard of self-employed individuals who have applied for PPP (Paycheck Protection Program) loans and were denied because they did not have business accounts. Ideally, you would have a checking and savings account set up for your business and use the savings account to stash money for your taxes. This will help you to keep this money safe until quarterly taxes are due, preventing you from accidentally spending it. As they say, failure to plan is planning to fail!

Insurance

Depending on the type of business you operate, you may need to consider insurance coverage. If you do not already have a professional liability policy, you may need to consider obtaining one. Other types of insurance will be dependent on the type of your business. Consult a trusted insurance professional to determine what type of coverage you may need.

Pricing

When considering a pricing strategy understand that you will need to clearly identify who your customer is. Having a clear idea of who your customer is will help you when determining your pricing strategy. You will need to figure out how what you offer is of value, understanding that value is in the eyes of the customer. Regardless of what your product or service is, you will not make a sale unless a customer values your offering.

Determine how much you will charge and establish your contract/customer agreement. If you are in a position where you have peers or family members who are self-employed, they can be a valuable resource to you. Ask them how they determined what they charge. I was already in the industry so I had an idea of what my rate would be, but if you are venturing into a new area you will need to shop around.

There is no one size fits all for pricing strategies. Depending on the client, you may be able to charge an hourly rate for piece work or may opt to charge a flat rate for projects, or a flat rate retainer fee. There will be a fine line between overcharging and undercharging in the case of flat rates. Sometimes in these scenarios, you may work more in one month which lowers the average hourly rate than you would in a different month. Another factor to consider is that if your work requires you to devote large blocks of time to one customer, this may prohibit you from working on other customer's work at the same time.

Example:

For XYZ customer, if you charged the client $4,000 as a flat rate per month for working on various projects, you may find that you worked 80 hours for this client in January. After you deduct $1200 for taxes (30%), you can pay yourself $2800, which equals $35 per hour for 80 hours of work. If next month, for this same customer you charged $4000 as a flat rate, you only worked 30 hours, (less $1200 for taxes), your hourly rate would be $93.

Take the same customer and assume that you negotiated an hourly rate for work instead of a flat rate. Remember the 30% rule for taxes when considering what you will charge. An hourly rate may be a more feasible and customer-friendly option for a client, although it can cost them greatly should you work more hours than they anticipated that you would. In addition, this option may appeal to a client to whom you do not have an established relationship. Your pricing strategy should not be all wins for either you or your client, but definitely look out for yourself!

When creating your customer agreements (contract for service), clearly delineate the scope of services for the agreement. You want your arrangement to be clear to both parties involved regardless as to what type of pricing is involved. Scope creep can happen and will create an uncomfortable situation. Be very clear as to what will be performed for the agreed upon rate.

* I am stopping here to put in a disclaimer. I am not an attorney. Please consider an attorney for questions regarding binding contracts. Do your research. Consult with mentors and legal counsel as you are able.

The above example covers a flat rat or hourly rate for a service provided assuming you are the service. Pricing might be different if there is an actual product involved. Factors that will need to be considered include costs to manufacture said product and other fixed costs. The most common pricing strategies are cost-based, customer-based and competition-based pricing.

Cost-based pricing includes the cost to provide a service or product and a markup. The markup is used to make a profit. An example would be a pair of scrubs which cost 15% to make, with a 50% markup which converts to a profit of $7.50. The scrubs then cost $22.50.

Customer-based pricing is essentially pricing based on what a customer is willing to pay, or the perceived value to the customer. Sometimes in this model, customers are charged a different rate for the same product. It is important when using a customer-based pricing model that you are still able to cover your costs, after all your goal is to make a profit.

Competition-based pricing is a model in which you have based your pricing on what your competitors are charging. This model works well to make sure that you are competitive, however, it does not take into consideration the value that your product might have over the competition.

For example, Heather Wilson, RN provides a personalized foot care service. When determining her charge per customer, she needs to determine what foot care supplies (disposables and non-disposables) she needs, what other costs go into her business (such as travel), and professional liability insurance. She then needs to decide what she wants her profit margin to be, and the amount of time it takes to provide her personalized service to each customer. In a personalized service business, each customer is buying your time, and your time is money.

Heather's research began by determining what a client was paying to go to a salon for foot care services, just as if you and I were to go to a salon for a pedicure. She then researched what a client would pay a podiatrist for in-office foot services, as these services are not typically covered by Medicare. She used a combination of a customer-based pricing strategy and a competition-based strategy to determine her price. Heather could have charged a premium for her service as she was offering more service by traveling to her clients, but she decided to price her service somewhere in the middle of a salon service and a podiatry service. This strategy gave her a competitive edge as she was focusing on how to provide value to her clients and give them exactly what they wanted. There are many factors to consider when setting up your pricing strategy. Bottom line is you can lose money and you will not make money if you don't price just right.

Now that you have an idea of how pricing works, understand that a good accounting system is necessary for keeping track of every sale and every expense of your business.

Bookkeeping/Accounting

Maintaining good documentation for your business is very important. Excel is a good tool for maintaining a spreadsheet. If you are not well versed in Excel, you can ask a friend or family member who is good with Excel to get you setup.

Alternatively, you may choose to elicit the help of a bookkeeper or accountant to set up financial spreadsheets for recording your revenue and expenses. The spreadsheet will be invaluable if used properly to record monthly revenue and expenses, allowing you to track every dollar. At tax time, a well-documented spreadsheet, along with the corresponding receipts for expenses, will make tax preparation less burdensome. Keeping up with these items monthly, entering them into the spreadsheet and filing the documents safely will keep you from scrambling before the filing deadlines arrive. Headaches averted!

There are software products available in addition to Excel such as QuickBooks and Wave that can be useful in creating and tracking professional looking invoices for your customers. Many of these require a paid subscription, so these are not fully necessary in the beginning stages. Excel will work for you if you have some knowledge or can get assistance.

However, having the proper price and spreadsheets setup will not help you if you have no customers.

Marketing Materials and Advertising

Determine what types of marketing materials you wish to have. Will they be print, a website, a brochure? There are many vendors available for making business cards, brochures, etc. Start with a small supply as there is no sense in spending large amounts of money initially. I recommend visiting a library for books on marketing, as well as attending any free webinars such as those offered through the SBA.

Networking will be an essential part of getting yourself out there. Meeting people in your community who can spread the word about your business is important. The local Chamber of Commerce in your community and online meetings such as Meetup, Eventbrite, and Facebook groups, are all good mechanisms to support your marketing efforts. To build a customer base, people need to know about your business.

How do you build a customer base? You build a customer base by getting the word out. Create a pitch that you can use to promote you and your business. The pitch needs to be less than a minute, ideally 30 seconds, and concise without bragging. Everyone you encounter while networking needs to know about your business, so you need to have a well-rehearsed pitch you can recite in your sleep.

In regards to a website, there are many options for web design and many are user-friendly, enabling you to design them yourself if you choose. Of course, you can also hire someone to develop your website but this may cost you $400-$1,000.

In our current world, it is imperative that you develop some sort of online media presence. You will need to determine what your presence will look like and if you will pay additional monies for a premium membership.

LinkedIn, Facebook, and Instagram can be valuable aids in getting the word out about your business. Most of these profiles are easy to set up and can be done without much technical knowledge.

CHAPTER 5-LEARN FROM YOURSELF

None of us are perfect. Our journey through life is impacted by the decisions we make and the actions we take because of these decisions. Opportunities to grow both personally and professionally are a result of the decisions we make, and what we learn at sometimes an unfortunate price. I say this from firsthand experience. I have made decisions that at the time seemed like the right thing to do. Upon reflection, maybe some of the decisions were not the best, but at least I took away from them either a new perspective or the scar of a lesson learned.

From a business perspective, I prefer to refer to mistakes as opportunities, removing the negative connotation that the word "mistake" tends to infer. Opportunities give you the chance to take away what works and does not work for your business. Take these opportunities to adapt your practices, attitudes, and approach based on previous outcomes.

Keep a journal of what is working and what is not working. To be successful in your business, you will need to constantly evolve practices to meet the needs of yourself, your business, and your customers.

No one is your friend when it comes to money. When it comes to business, no one is your friend. Even if you enter a contract to perform your business for a friend of yours, know that when it comes to money, NO ONE IS YOUR FRIEND.

Consider the situation in which your friend can negotiate contracts and services for his or her employer and he/she signs your contract. What if your friend gets fired, demoted, or even quits their job? Will you then have to chase down payments? Will your contract be terminated? These are things to keep in mind. A well-documented contract will help you outline a termination clause so that the customer cannot fire you without proper notice in a situation like this. The perception that something is OK because they are your friend will not help you and may damage that relationship. Always get everything in writing so that there will be no misunderstandings which can leave someone with hurt feelings, or a hurt bank account.

Payment up front. For some new customers, if the contract work requires extensive preparation along with travel, consideration should be made for a partial payment at the signing of the contract. This can offset some of the business expenses and be especially helpful in the beginning. A partial payment also gives you a little peace of mind when performing work for a customer whom you do not already have an established relationship with.

Late fees. Businesses have expenses that need to be covered. Chasing down payments from clients is an unpleasant and awkward predicament. Building a late fee into your contract may be just enough to deter delinquent payments. These can be either in the form of a flat rate or as a percentage of the total invoice. You may decide to assess the late fee for every month past due as a deterrent for late payments. A typical late fee I might charge would range from 2-5% of the invoice amount. You can make this late fee any amount that you wish, and obviously the larger the dollar amount of the invoice, the more substantial a late fee penalty might be.

Insufficient Funds Charges. Another uncomfortable situation that can happen is bank charges for insufficient funds. For returned check charges, a suggestion is to charge an additional fee for any instance in which a payment is returned due to insufficient funds. This charge will be assessed for the inconvenience of a returned check and is charged along with a late fee if the payment is now late due to the NSF charge. Make sure that the insufficient funds charge covers, at a minimum, the amount that your bank will charge you for the returned check.

   *As a side note here, I do not use customer payments to pay any business expenses or payroll expenses until I know the check has cleared the bank. I give a payment a good 10 days to clear before I use that money for expenses.

Rates. If you are a service-based business and charge an hourly rate for your work, consider charging one rate for a set number of hours for services rendered (i.e. up to 40 hours worked) and a different rate for additional hours worked, such as an overtime rate for hours in excess of the set hours. Other things to consider would be to charge an additional rate for work performed after hours, such as weekends or holidays.

Scope of the project. Consider the scope of the project and understand that there is no one-size-fits-all approach. In quoting a rate for services, it is helpful to have a good feel for what the project entails to make sure you are not undercharging, which costs you money and time. You also don't want to be overcharging which could cause you to lose customers.

Cancellation clauses. Are you able to terminate the contract immediately if the need dictates (non-payment, continual late payments, gross misconduct, etc.)? If you are in a contract which requires excessive preparation, time, travel, and resources on your part, consider drafting a termination clause which requires that the client must pay you for the remaining balance of the terms of the contract for situations that could arise in which you may desire to terminate the contract immediately (as in the instance of gross misconduct for example).

Journal/Keep Notes. My use of a journal has helped me keep notes of what has worked and what hasn't worked well. In many ways, the journal helps me keep track of the things I wish I would have known on the first few go arounds with my customers.

Your time is money. It is easy to undercharge a client just to get clients, but this won't necessarily sustain you. Carefully consider your pricing strategy but allow room for flexibility.

Entrepreneurial Truths that I have learned:

The primary barrier to success is fear; fear of taking the first step. Feel the fear and move on anyway.

Fear of growth will keep you stagnant. You will have to constantly grow in your business. Even once your business is up and running, you will need to periodically reevaluate it to remain relevant and tailor it to the needs of your customer.

Always think about reinvention. Reinvent your product, service, and your process. What worked for your entrepreneurial journey at one point, may not be the direction you should continue in.

Accept rejection when you take the risk. Rejection happens.

Failure is a part of life and always has been. Grow from it.

Do not compare your success with someone else's.

Stop the negative self-talk.

Be clear as to your reason. Make sure you are starting this business for the right reason.

CHAPTER 6- CLOSING

While this book is not a complete manual for starting a business, I hope that for those who have read it, you have gained a little hope for your situation. You are only stuck if you choose to be stuck. One step forward is progress, and little by little, with the right planning, research, and mentorship, you will find the strength to move to a more fulfilling path.

There will never be a perfect time to start a business. While it is true that you will need to adequately and thoughtfully prepare, avoid allowing your preparation to turn into procrastination. If you truly desire to have your own business, understand that risks will always exist and move forward in acceptance.

Accept that there will be successes and failures. Businesses fail, products or services that you attempt to offer through your business might fail. With the pandemic, we have seen many small businesses, and even many large industries, completely tank. If a large industry can tank, you can bet that a small business can too. This should not stop you if you have the desire and courage to weather the storms. You may have to change your business model and develop new business relationships, but failure can and does affect any type of venture. Do not allow the risk of failure to keep you from creating a better career for yourself.

I encourage you to keep your spirits up, find inspiration in knowing that anything is possible once you figure out what your "thing" is.

Best of luck to you!

CHAPTER 7-INTERVIEWS
REAL LIFE NURSE ENTREPRENEURS

Entrepreneur: Michelle Podlesni, RN, CEO President of National Nurses in Business Association (NNBA)

UNconventional Nurse® Going from Burnout to Bliss! Founder & Author

Bloom Service Group, LLC. CEO & President

Contact info:
mdp@nursesbusiness.com,
michelle@unconventionalnurse.com

phone (877) 353 – 8888

NNBA Nurses in Business
P.O. Box 777951
Henderson, NV 89052

Website:
www.NursesBusiness.com (NNBA)
www.UNconventionalNurse.com –
UNconventional Nurse®

How long has your business been in existence?

I have been an entrepreneur since the 90's, a serial entrepreneur with several different businesses. I still promote that nurses should not have all their eggs in one basket. I started UNconventional Nurse® as a blog in 2011. Writing a book was always on my bucket list so I wrote *UNconventional Nurse: Going from Burnout to Bliss!* In it I shared with nurses the 10 Steps I learned and used while I was a corporate executive, and the president of a major software company. I wrote *UNconventional Nurse* for nurses because I could see that nurses were under-served, devalued, and overworked. It hurt me to see nurses, in a profession I loved, not being happy in their jobs. The level of burnout was rising to 35% and this was well before COVID-19. I wanted to help in the best way I was able and that was to share with nurses the business strategies, skill sets, and examples that I knew could change the trajectory of their careers and their life. It was nurse's responses to this book (becoming #1 Amazon bestseller in nursing) and my coaching programs that led the past president of the National Nurses in Business Association, NNBA, to call me and request that I speak at their annual conference on nurse entrepreneurship. I delivered my speech in October of 2013. Shortly after this, I was recruited to become NNBA's new president. I have been the president of the NNBA for the past seven years.

What was the turning point which caused you to travel down the entrepreneurial path? Was there a defining moment?

My turning point was just like so many nurses today. Burnout was the turning point. I was working swing shifts, weekends, and holidays. I had been in nursing for 10 years and I just wanted to feel 'normal' because I felt so out of step with my friends and family. I really wanted to experience a job where I could work 9-5 and have weekends off. I started checking the paper for just about anything else. I did not know one nurse that was not working in a traditional environment. I found a group health insurance company, Bankers Life, that was looking for a healthcare resource specialist. I applied, interviewed, and the rest is history. This was my first encounter with using computers and I turned into a nurse nerd, loving how I could analyze healthcare data, see trends, and be able to make recommendations to patients and their families.

Regarding the journey, how long did it take you to get from concept to execution?

This is an interesting question, so I must break it up by businesses. We started our Senior Care company in 2002 and we sold it in 2010. There were seventy caregivers, administrative staff, and recurring clients. I started UNconventional Nurse® in 2011 and it is on-going. It was profitable in 2013 with book sales, speaking engagements, coaching programs, and workshops. The National Nurses in Business Association, NNBA, was founded in 1985 and continues in execution with on-going innovation and services in memberships, conferences, products, and speaking engagements.

I have been a paid Consultant, Business Advisor, and Medical Billing Cost Containment Expert for the past thirty years and continue to work with corporate clients.

If you could give one piece of advice to a peer interested in embarking on the journey, what would that piece of advice be?

Cultivate and nurture support systems. Entrepreneurship can be lonely. You will need to surround yourself with people who believe in your dreams and support them. From a professional standpoint, there are many organizations that can support and encourage you. Many nurses attribute their membership in the National Nurses in Business Association, NNBA, as being pivotal to their success as an entrepreneur. They can see concrete examples of nurses that have made the transition to business and are resources available to answer questions. Members have made life-long friends and have worked on many collaborative projects. There are supportive organizations that are specific specialties within nursing and outside nursing. For example, I used to be a member of the American Board of Quality Assurance and Utilization Review and I've been a member of various Chamber of Commerce's and local area business networking groups. All are invaluable to providing support and resources.

I've grown several successful corporations and businesses. My nursing education and experience set the foundation for me achieving success beyond what I ever dreamed was possible. Did I make mistakes? Too many to count, and every day I am learning. But this I know; nurses make great business owners. My best piece of advice is cultivate and nurture your support systems. Relationships are everything and much study on our well-being supports this. Having solid personal and professional communities will help you get on the right track; it will open doors and provide resources. You can achieve all the other lessons in business *just by getting started in business*. However, personal and professional support is what will sustain you. And then you will have a great cheering section!

Company: Frontier Health & Resources
Entrepreneur: Joey Ferry, BSN, RN
(Co-Founder)

Contact info:
Joey@frontierhealthresources.com

Website: www.safeseizure.com

How long has your business been in existence?
Established in 2017. Products in the market since 2019.

What was the turning point which caused you to travel down the entrepreneurial path? Was there a defining moment?
   I'm an entrepreneur at heart. I grew up in a family of owner-operated truck drivers where I got to watch my dad and his brothers grow their business from one truck to a full fleet. Like many others, from a very young age I explored business and entrepreneurship in creative ways. From buying candy at wholesale prices and reselling to friends at school to creating my own lottery raffle in the 6th grade (that got shut down very quick).

   When asked where I'd be in 10 years for the senior yearbook, my reply was "I'll own my own business." That was until my freshman year in college where a science teacher and retired nurse told me all about nursing; it pays well, job security, flexible scheduling, rewarding; etc. Concerned with the stability of business which is filled with uncertainty and risk, I opted for a path in nursing. However, the entrepreneurial itch never went away.

During the first few years of my nursing career I attempted multiple businesses (completely unrelated to healthcare) from a sports drink, mobile app, and everything in between. Although not a single idea was successful, I gained invaluable knowledge and experience that would later help me gain success in the business world.

I spent 12 years of my nursing career at the bedside as a night shift Float Pool nurse. One night I was floated to a unit where I met a young energetic nurse named Taofiki (toe-fee-key). He and I spent the entire shift talking about technology and the frustrations of healthcare's lack of technology. Hospitals are time machines with the dial set 10 years back. Throughout our conversation we talked about our various passions, previous business ventures, and my active role in our hospital system, which included sitting on the product review committee. That morning, Taofiki asked to talk to me outside of work. We went to a local coffee shop where he went on to show me a "product" he was ready to pitch and sell to the hospital. Although Taofiki's product was unrefined and not ready to sell, he had identified a real problem in nursing- the way we pad bed rails for patients on seizure precautions. That day, SafeSeizure™ was born.

Regarding the journey, how long did it take you to get from concept to execution?

Within 24 hours, Taofiki and I had revamped his pre-existing idea to a full-fledged product design concept. For the next few weeks, we sourced material for the different elements of our idea. We purchased an inflatable camping pad from Amazon and cut straps off an old backpack. Taofiki took straps and the pad to a local dry-cleaning shop and had them sewn together. Voilà!

We then began seeking manufactures to make an official prototype. With a refined prototype in hand, we approached our current hospital system with a request to trial the product. After a comprehensive review of the product demo our hospital agreed to a 3-month trial.

Nurses loved the product! We received an overwhelmingly positive review of the product with staff continuously asking for more

SafeSeizure™ pads. After almost a year of sifting through all the legal red tape of two employees with a product, we were finally approved as a vendor and began selling our first product. Since then, we have grown to include 6 hospital systems with several other hospitals actively trialing the product. Recently, Kaiser Permanente has approved the product for use in all of their hospitals nationwide. In addition, our product allowed us to win the 2020 ANA Innovations Award Powered by BD along with two Nightingale Awards for Innovation (2019 and 2020).

If you could give one piece of advice to a peer interested in embarking on the journey, what would that piece of advice be?

Getting a product or idea from A to Z can be very difficult and time consuming. Each step of the way will present different challenges and roadblocks. Some of which, can feel virtually impossible to accomplish and discourage you from moving forward. If this happens at step A, B, or C, you'll never get anywhere, or worse, never even start. If this happens at step W, X, or Y, you've potentially wasted a ton of time, money, and energy.

Always think about Z. In fact, romance about Z. How amazing would it be if Z!? If Z were possible, it would change the world!

When times get tough or you get discouraged,
Z will keep you motivated and on track.

Some say I spend too much time with my
head in the clouds, I say, I like the view.

Company: Everyday Divinity, LLC and The Foot and Nail Institute LLC

**Entrepreneur: Heather Wilson, RN CFCS
Contact info:**
customerservice@everydaydivinity.com

Phone 614-716-9919
support@footandnailinstitute.com

Website:
www.EverydayDivinity.com
www.footandnailinstitute.com **(coming soon)**

How long has your business been in existence?

I started Everyday Divinity in 2011 after seeing the lack of appropriate routine foot care services available in the marketplace to our senior demographic. I worked on a vascular floor in the hospital where I saw the rise of foot infections as well as amputations taking place. This was due to the lack of foot care resources available. Seniors began seeking salon pedicures for the simple act of toenail trimmings that they themself were no longer able to perform. Insurance restrictions were driving podiatrists away from performing the service, leaving a gap that needed to be filled within the healthcare system. Nurses are a perfect solution to fill this gap!

What was the turning point which caused you to travel down the entrepreneurial path? Was there a defining moment?

I wanted more out of life both professionally and personally. The healthcare sector was ever-changing. Longer hours, less resources, and more bureaucracy made it difficult to deliver the care I prided myself on. Healthcare was going in a direction where I started to question the integrity of the care I was delivering as a nurse. That did not sit well with me. I believe it's the reason why nurse burnout is so high today.

Regarding the journey, how long did it take you to get from concept to execution?

A good full 2+ years to sort out the trails & errors of the business. I had taken 2 foot care courses in that time yet I was still left with so many questions regarding the execution of the foot care business. Which is why I have created The Foot and Nail Institute. I wanted to offer nurses the opportunity to learn the business of foot care from a nurse who had been doing it successfully for 10 years. I wanted to provide them a process that they could duplicate in their own marketplace. Nurses can take our online course to learn the business of foot care as well as learn how to execute a foot care clinic. They can come train with me for hands-on training also in my clinic. I want every nurse who takes our course to be successful because they deserve it! I also know the need for foot care across the nation is so great which is why I am offering a membership option to increase their opportunity of success. Together we will walk down the path of business ownership beyond just the course.

If you could give one piece of advice to a peer interested in embarking on the journey, what would that piece of advice be?

I would say do your research about the opportunities that are out there. Look to organizations such as the NNBA, National Nurse Business Association, to find different nurse owned businesses. Also start by determining if you want a side hustle or a whole hustle? There is a big difference.

Company: CathWear
Entrepreneur:
Brian O. Mohika, BSN, RN, CEO, Inventor,
Author

Contact info: Brian.mohika@cathwear.com

Website: www.cathwear.com

New Book: Let It Flow, One Nurse's Entrepreneurial Journey

How long has your business been in existence?

The business has been open for 2 years, selling on our website (cathwear.com and on Amazon).

What was the turning point which caused you to travel down the entrepreneurial path? Was there a defining moment?

The journey started with an identified need for a product not already in existence. The defining moment was when I quit on my first invention and then someone else invented it. I used it as motivation to never quit again.

Regarding the journey, how long did it take you to get from concept to execution?

The total elapsed time was 6 years.

If you could give one piece of advice to a peer interested in embarking on the journey, what would that piece of advice be?

Do not lead with emotions and do not quit on your dreams.

Company: Case Management Institute and The Stay At Home Nurse

Entrepreneur: Deanna Cooper Gillingham RN, CCM

Website:
CaseManagementInstitute.com
thestayathomenurse.com

How long has your business been in existence?

The Stay At Home Nurse was started in December 2013. The Case Management Institute started in 2018.

What was the turning point which caused you to travel down the entrepreneurial path? Was there a defining moment?

I finally had what I thought was the perfect job. I was working from home, had autonomy in the day to day of my work, was respected by my peers and management, was making more money than I ever had, and was making an impact on the clients I served. Yet I still felt like something was missing, my freedom. I still did not have the freedom to work the hours I wanted, as much or as little as I wanted, from anywhere I wanted. I could not take vacation without asking permission. And I was still trading time for dollars. I knew the only way to truly get everything I wanted was to become an entrepreneur.

Regarding the journey, how long did it take you to get from concept to execution?

I spent 3 months looking over different opportunities and weighing the pros and cons. I evaluated the opportunities by their potential to get me to where I wanted to be, in control of all aspects of my life. I also evaluated whether I would enjoy the journey. After 3 months I made the choice to start a company that would educate other case managers and help them to get their certification.

It took an additional year of daily researching and writing while working my full-time job to write the book that would become my first product and publish it.

If you could give one piece of advice to a peer interested in embarking on the journey, what would that piece of advice be?

Find someone who is where you want to be and learn from them.

Company: **Prosurgassist**
Entrepreneur: **Dale Vladic, RN, CNOR, CRNFA**
Contact: Prosurgassist@aol.com

How long has your business been in existence?

I have been in the medical field since 1983. I started out as a Surgical Technologist, then graduated nursing school in 1990. I have always worked exclusively in the surgical setting and have started practicing as a Surgical Assistant within three months of graduating my Surgical Technologist program.

I Provide Freelance Surgical Assistant services to Hospitals, Ambulatory Surgical Centers, Surgeons in all surgical settings including in-office advanced procedure rooms, in addition to offering services and any other surgical setting.

What was the turning point which caused you to travel down the entrepreneurial path? Was there a defining moment?

From my first day (October 10, 1983) in the operating room even as a student, I witnessed the autonomy of the surgical assistant role and sought to achieve self-employment and owning my own freelance practice as a Surgical Assistant.

Regarding the journey, how long did it take you to get from concept to execution?
Approximately 20 years. This was because I felt that to be successful, I needed to be extremely skilled and highly experienced to provide quality services and care to the patients and settings I would be working in. I also needed to build respect and trust, as well as having a reputation by my peers to be respected for my abilities in the community. I valued experience very highly as a means to gaining a reputation for quality to be a key factor to successfully owning my own freelance practice. I spent the first 20 years building the foundation that supported the above described qualities.

The actual build up phase took approximately 7 months because of the nature of my business model and hard-earned reputation I was successful getting work almost immediately. However, the income stream was slower to develop. I have also modified and refined the structure of my practice to meet the needs of my accounts and clients over the 16 years I have been in practice.

If you could give one piece of advice to a peer interested in embarking on the journey, what would that piece of advice be?

Always have a backup plan. I do other activities and have sideline businesses that if needed could replace my practice should the government and or the medical industry legislate my business model out of existence. I would advise those who insist on medical or nursing entrepreneurship to protect themselves in the same manner.

Company Name: Bells Coaching
Entrepreneur: Sarah Bell, MBA, BSN, RN
Website: www.bellscoaching.com
Email: sarah.bell@bellscoaching.com

How long has your business been in existence?
8 years.

What was the turning point which caused you to travel down the entrepreneurial path? Was there a defining moment?
It was tough to let go of the regular paycheck. In the end, I wasn't happy, and the turning point was when I realized I was not going to have the impact I wanted unless I left my job.

Regarding the journey, how long did it take you to get from concept to execution?
This has been a long journey. I have been planning and stargazing, making mistakes, changing my mind, etc, for 8 years. When I finally made the decision in Sept 2020 to quit my job it has taken me 5 months to get ready to sell my programs.

If you could give one piece of advice to a peer interested in embarking on the journey, what would that piece of advice be?

Follow your heart, trust in your ability, and get support. Doing it alone is lonely and takes a lot longer.

Company:
The Bridge RN Patient Advocates
Entrepreneur: Melissa Cardine MSN, RN,
WOCN, BCPA
Website: www.TheBridgeRN.com
The Bridge Health Advocates:
www.BridgeHealthAdvocates.com

How long has your business been in existence?

The Bridge RN Patient Advocates since 2015 and The Bridge Health Advocates since 2019.

What was the turning point which caused you to travel down the entrepreneurial path? Was there a defining moment?

My favorite part of being a nurse is listening to patients' stories. Along with listening to them and their families I enjoy collaborating with other healthcare professionals to figure out what is going on and help come up with a plan. I like talking with physicians, nurses, therapists, social workers, dieticians, and other healthcare professionals trying to better understand what is going on with the patient. I ask questions. I also really like coming up with solutions. Unfortunately, in the role I had as a nurse I was not able to do this the way I envisioned. I created The Bridge RN Patient

Advocates to practice the type of nursing I imagined.

For those unfamiliar, a patient advocate can assist a patient with navigating their illnesses and conditions by working closely with them to identify their needs through an assessment and medication reviews. Furthermore, an advocate assists by attending doctor visits as requested, making calls on the patient's behalf, and by providing the patient with self-confidence in making informed decisions about their care.

Regarding the journey, how long did it take you to get from concept to execution?
    I had thought about starting a patient advocacy business for years. Once I made up my mind that this is what I wanted to do it only took me 3 months. The hard part was making up my mind and just doing it.

If you could give one piece of advice to a peer interested in embarking on the journey, what would that piece of advice be?
    What is your passion? It is what will drive you to succeed and help you conquer any fears you have of failure. People will be attracted to your passion. They will feel your passion, your integrity, and want to be associated with you. Think about your education, experience, and expertise. Consider what you really enjoy

doing. What is going to get you out of bed in the morning? In a perfect world, how would you like to spend your days? What excites you?

Company Name:
Surgical Investors and Advisors and
LTD Healthcare Consultants LLC

Entrepreneur: Lacey T Dyer RN
Website: https://www.surgicalinvestors.com/

How long has your business been in existence?

I have been an SIA partner since 2018. LTD Healthcare Consultants has been in existence since 2015

What was the turning point which caused you to travel down the entrepreneurial path? Was there a defining moment?

I began feeling discontent with the management of surgery centers. After being overlooked for a higher management opportunity, I took a course by Max Lucado called "Finding your sweet spot." After a year of frustration and not enjoying my job, my spouse encouraged me to search for new opportunities. The course helped me define what parts of my career I enjoyed the most. I learned that I like the startup of new projects and then become bored with the day in/day out of management.

LTD Healthcare Consultants was started as an opportunity to develop speaking opportunities and individual projects that might come my way aside from my partnership.

Regarding the journey, how long did it take you to get from concept to execution?
The transition to partnership occurred after 2 years with the company. Upon hire, I had verbalized that my interest was in ownership, not an employee relationship. I was of value and wanted them to know I was invested in the success of the team for the long run.

If you could give one piece of advice to a peer interested in embarking on the journey, what would that piece of advice be?
Do not underestimate your value. Start early in your career looking at your unique skills and what you enjoy.

Company: JobDocs, LLC
Entrepreneur: Lisa Porter MSN, RN, FNP-BC
Website: https://jobdocs.net

How long has your business been in existence?
4 years.

What was the turning point which caused you to travel down the entrepreneurial path? Was there a defining moment?
There are so many. I love this quote from a course I took at Stanford Online- Startup School. "If you fail to do/create/build this, you're depriving the world of something great. And you're not living up to your own potential."

Regarding the journey, how long did it take you to get from concept to execution?
This is a hard question to answer because execution means different things. I would say for a business, the true measure of execution is that you have customers and revenue so the answer for JobDocs would be about 2 years. There were a lot of steps that led up to that. Here is a brief timeline...
5/19/16 Idea for an app
7/26/16 Submitted concept idea to tech competition (didn't win but was in top 10% of

submission. Feedback: Idea is great, need to learn business)

9/13/16 Met software developer
10/12/16 Met with business mentor
10/14/16 Met with design team, created interactive prototype focused on user experience. Goal: Feedback
12/11/16 App development begins
12/27/16 Official "Business" with license
10/2017 Joined a business incubator
7/5/18 App launched in Google Play and App Store

JobDocs is an application which can serve as a safe place to store all your important documents such BLS, ACLS, licensure, training information so that you always have access and can keep up with the expiration dates.

If you could give one piece of advice to a peer interested in embarking on the journey, what would that piece of advice be?
Before you invest money, invest your time meeting with as many people as you can-future customers, mentors, fellow entrepreneurs. Do not just "connect." Build relationships with people that will support you in your journey. Then find trusted advisors

(legal, financial, business, etc) that will guide
(and protect) you on your entrepreneurial path.

Company Name:
The Ketamine Academy
The IV Therapy Academy
The Healthcare Entrepreneur Academy Podcast

Entrepreneur: LCDR Jason A. Duprat, MBA, MSA

Website:
http://www.ketamineacademy.com/
http://www.ivtherapyacademy.com/

How long has your business been in existence?

The Ketamine Academy was started in 2017 and the IV Therapy Academy was started in 2018. Both businesses are designed to assist physicians and advanced level nurses (NPs and CRNAs) establish infusion therapy practices.

What was the turning point which caused you to travel down the entrepreneurial path? Was there a defining moment?

Yes, when I was in anesthesia (CRNA) school I realized that I was accumulating a large amount of student debt. Upon finishing school, I often worked extra to help pay down the debt. I was working all the time, picking up extra shifts, working on nights and weekends, sacrificing my personal time. I realized that I would need to find a way to make additional money without sacrificing so much. I started listening to the *Entrepreneurs on Fire* podcasts and began thinking of ideas. In 2015, an ER physician was referred to me by a friend. This physician was wanting the perspective of an anesthesia provider regarding starting a ketamine clinic.

Regarding the journey, how long did it take you to get from concept to execution?

I started my ketamine research on starting a ketamine therapy practice in 2016 almost a year after the call with that physician, so it took me 1 year to get the practice running. I launched the practice a few months after JAMA Psychiatry published their consensus guidelines on the use of ketamine therapy for depression. A couple of months after opening the practice I started the Ketamine Academy to fill the unmet need for ketamine therapy training and continuing education.

If you could give one piece of advice to a peer interested in embarking on the journey, what would that piece of advice be?

There are really three key pieces of advice that I would give:

1. You must have a burning desire to be an entrepreneur to keep you focused on the

outcome. Ideally you are someone who enjoys autonomy.

2. You must have discipline and be a driven person. It would be easy as an entrepreneur to lack structure since you do not have a boss to report to. Structure is key to keep you on track.

3. You must have resilience. The road can be long and winding with obstacles along the way designed to stop you. You will get slowed down and may be moving at 1 mph, but you must stay focused and be able to bounce back.

REFERENCES AND HELPFUL WEBSITES

The Internal Revenue Service-Government agency with valuable information regarding applying for a TAX ID/EIN, 1099 contractor vs employee definitions, information regarding various types of business formats to include the LLC, C-corp, etc.
https://www.irs.gov/

National Nurses In Business Association-Membership organization for nurse entrepreneurs, with conferences, a newsletter, and resources for nurse business owners.
https://nursesbusiness.com/

SCORE-Organization providing mentors, resources, webinars for entrepreneurs.
https://www.score.org/

Small Business Administration-U.S. Government supported organization offering webinars, articles, learning tools and mentorship for starting a small business.
https://www.sba.gov/

Recommended Books:

Drain, Patricia Noel. *Discovering your Core* (2019). A book on self discovery.

Allen, Dr. Kathleen and Economy, Peter. *The Complete MBA for Dummies* (2000). Tips on various business topics.

www.ingramcontent.com/pod-product-compliance
Lightning Source LLC
Chambersburg PA
CBHW060621200326

41521CB00007B/842